WOODY AND JUNE
VERSUS THE EX

WOODY AND JUNE VERSUS THE EX

WOODY AND JUNE VERSUS THE APOCALYPSE,
EPISODE 4

ROBERT J. MCCARTER

LITTLE HUMMINGBIRD PUBLISHING

WOODY AND JUNE
VERSUS
THE APOCALYPSE

CHAPTER ONE

I THINK June used to be an Army Ranger or something. Not that I know exactly what an Army Ranger is, and this being post-zombie-apocalypse Arizona, I can't exactly look it up on my smartphone.

She is lying on the sand, her hunting rifle propped up on her backpack, sighting a straggler from the zombie horde that chased us down into the Grand Canyon. We're on a sand island in the middle of the Colorado River under the hot spring sun. We swam over two days ago to save our sweet, fresh brains. The Zs tried to follow but got swept downstream.

I've given up on the idea of her being an Israeli secret agent with Mossad, despite her olive complexion and blue eyes. The little Spanish I've heard her speak is perfect, lacking the usual sloppy American accent. I can't speak Spanish properly—I've got that sloppy American accent—but I know when it's spoken properly.

"There, Woody," she says. "Can you see it?"

I'm sitting next to her looking through my binoculars, trying desperately to focus on the beautiful desert landscape of the Grand Canyon and not on the gorgeous pixie woman lying next to me. "Yup. I see it. One zombie tourist wandering around the— oh... he walks right into a prickly pear cactus and keeps on going, a couple of 'em clinging to his leg. The poor guy lost his flip-flops, but at least he's still got his fanny pack."

I briefly considered that she might be a spy from Spain or Mexico —no idea what their intelligence agencies are called—but discard that too. She's just too American.

"I can take him," she says, even though he's at least a hundred yards off.

So that leaves me with something like Green Beret or Army Ranger. Although the idea of ending up post-apocalypse with an international spy is rather... intriguing, the mystery of June is intriguing enough without that.

"Yeah you can," I say, "but how about we save the ammo, and keep a low profile." We're just downstream from some rapids, so we haven't been worried about conversation attracting attention, but a gunshot definitely could.

She nods and sits up, brushing the sand from her T-shirt. It's hot, so she's down to a T-shirt and undies, as am I.

See why I'm distracted?

"We polluted the Grand Canyon with Zs," she says, shaking her head.

I nod. "Yeah. Sucks. I think a lot of them washed to shore after chasing us and are just wandering now."

This is day eight of Woody and June versus the End of the World and our second day on this sand island. The trip down involved a lot of bushwalking, a lot of miles, and some very close calls. We've been resting and letting our blisters heal in this rare zombie-free zone.

"We can't stay much longer." She nods at our packs, the food we scrounged at Desert View Lookout is running thin. "What are we going to do, partner?" She looks at me with those beautiful blues of hers and I just want to melt... or kiss her. Yeah, kiss her is definitely the choice.

Our relationship has progressed nicely since we met up in Flagstaff. We've gone from wary, to saving each other's lives, to trust, to officially being partners when we made it to this island alive. I think mostly because she doesn't want to try to survive one more of my hair-brained schemes again without a discussion.

Me? I want all the June I can get. Every day, year-round, give me June, month after month. She's strong, smart, beautiful, and capable. Take any "gun-wielding female force to be reckoned with" from the movies and I'd put my money on her every time. Sarah Connor, no problem. Ellen Ripley, you bet. Dana Scully, pa-lease...

"At least they haven't found us with their fresh-brains zombie radar," I say with a grin.

She shakes her head. "But why not?"

"I've got a theory," I offer.

She rolls her eyes. I have a history with my theories, even in our short time together. My fungus/parasite theory of zombiedom has kind of checked out. My "time travelers did it to us to save the planet" theory of the origin of the infection hasn't gotten any traction.

"Please enlighten me," she says, taking a sip from her water bottle and scanning our surroundings for danger. It's a good habit to have.

There are several challenges here. I don't know if she's into me, or guys for that matter, and the apocalypse doesn't actually leave much time for romance, what with all the running from flesh-eating zombies and psychotic, petty, wannabe warlords.

My approach? Be nice. Be patient. Be charming... well, at least amusing. I can amuse, not at all sure if I can charm.

"So, fungus head zombies, check," I say. "We proved it with that poor dried up sap we dissected."

She nods.

"Super large horde had a super good sense of where we were. We couldn't lose them on the way down here despite putting some distance between us."

"Check," says.

"Singles," I say, pointing towards the one who we sighted just in time to watch him tumble into a wash, "not so good."

"Right..."

"Ergo, presto—" I say, doing a silly jazz-hands gesture.

"I don't think that is the way it goes," she says, one eyebrow arched.

"Presto...?" I wave my jazz hands again.

She shakes her head, but she's smiling, so that makes me happy.

"Ergo, the more zombies, the better their flesh detection ability. Their fungus minds must be more powerful together."

I stand up, doff my hat, and take a bow and she laughs. This puts me in a good place for my goals for a post-apocalyptic day. There's the laughter, and on our zombie-free island, survival seems assured. And I'm here with June, so that means it's a good day.

A shot rings out, the sound bouncing off the canyon walls, and June is back down on the sand scanning the terrain with the scope of her hunting rifle.

I hit the sand and start looking with my binocs.

Shit!

We're not the only living at the bottom of the Grand Canyon.

Yeah, I might have been a bit preliminary on that survival part.

CHAPTER TWO

WHAT'S next on the June and Woody hit-parade? Digging a long shallow hole in the sand under the hot Arizona sun, mounding the sand along the edge so it kinda looks like a natural bump from a distance, and lying in the hole—maybe trench is a better word—until dark.

This is June's idea, which adds another check to the "Army Ranger or some such thing" list.

The shot isn't that close, so we figured we have time. It is clear we need to leave. Our sand island is perfect for zombie protection, but we're sitting ducks for people with guns. Leaving in the middle of the day is not smart either and we don't have a plan yet, thus the digging like crazed gophers.

After all, it has been well established after our last close call on the shore of the river that all plans must be discussed. Most specifically any plan hatched out of my strange brain.

But hey, I get to lie down in the damp sand next to a beautiful woman for six hours. Not so bad, really.

"They're shooting our zombies," she says once we're settled in with our bodies and all our stuff below ground level. It won't help if folks are up high, but it will work for people close or on the trail.

"*Our* zombies? So, have we adopted them or something now?" I ask. "Are they our unruly children?"

"Shut up," she says, elbowing me in the ribs. The elbow is teasing but the tone is serious. Perhaps I should save the silliness until we survive this.

"Phantom Ranch is a long ways downstream," I say. "That would be the best place to hole up down here, but it's forty miles or so of hiking."

She sighs. "We never get a break, do we?"

I want to tell her that she's the biggest break I've had since the Zs started. Hell... maybe the biggest break ever. But I don't. This is not the time, but I resolve to find the time. This is just silly. I like her, I need to find out if she likes me.

"We got this, June," I say. "There are a lot of campsites along the Colorado that the river runners used. Maybe someone set up camp when there were no Zs down here. Now they're too busy fighting Zs to worry about us."

She nods and another shot rings out and I jump. We are in a canyon and sound will travel farther than in the open, so I really have no idea how far away they are.

"I'd say they're three miles away, give or take," she says. There goes another tick on the military trained bad-ass list.

This island is very shallow, the sand damp and blessedly cool. Our prone view of the world is pretty nice too, the blue sky above, scalloped reddish sandstone rising up. The lull of the rapids and the river. I want to take a nap, but we don't have a plan yet.

"Back the way we came?" I propose. "Up Tanner Trail, properly, no confronting five-hundred-foot cliffs. Over to Desert View, get our truck, and be merrily on our way? It will be a very long day, but the Zs are thinned out, so it should be doable."

"Good plan," she says, and she grabs my hand and squeezes it. "I'll take first watch if you want to snooze a bit."

Have I mentioned how completely awesome this woman is?

As I close my eyes and begin to drift, it occurs to me that in the pre-Z world, I wouldn't have stood a chance with this one. She's too... *everything*. And I'm... just a guy who can think on his feet and isn't an ass.

Even if she does like guys, I'm sure it's just not enough. She's way out of my league.

CHAPTER THREE

I'M ON LAST WATCH, sitting in our trench scanning our surroundings as the Colorado rushes past. It's in the low sixties and I am not looking forward to a dip in the forty-five-degree river.

The eastern horizon is just starting to lighten and it's time for me to wake June, but I hesitate. This moment here seems rare, almost holy.

The stars are bright above and the Canyon is indistinct shadows above us. I hear the roar of the rapids just upstream and the rush of the breeze against sandstone. June is breathing deep and steady and I take a deep breath of the cool, fresh air.

This moment is peace. It's almost like the apocalypse didn't happen and June and I are on a river trip camped out under the stars, happy and relaxed.

Like, maybe we've been together for a while and have just hit that point when you can start being yourself around your partner. You know, where you can both admit that you're human and not perfect.

Not quite to that been married forever and leave the bathroom door open and farting—as long as they're not real stinkers—is not a big deal, but a comfortable familiarity.

And June, despite my romantic ramblings, is not perfect. I still know almost nothing about her, and that is in part about keeping the past at arm's length—we've all lost so much—but there is more there. She's very guarded. She is good at survival, but is she good at anything beyond that? Are any of us at this point?

Before we met, I was a loner and was going through this life with nothing left to lose, nothing of value anyone would want to take from me.

June has changed all of that, but she's still such a mystery.

"June," I whisper. "Time for our nice cold bath."

She wakes with a start, her breath coming fast, her gun in hand before she even sits up. Her eyes are wide as she looks around, and then her gun is trained on me.

"It's okay, June," I say, my hands in front of me and my heart pounding. "It's just me, Woody. We need to get going."

She nods and is back to herself quickly. "Sorry," she says, rubbing at her eyes.

Maybe it's just the apocalypse that did this to her, the strain of daily survival. That's what I tell myself, anyway.

We split a can of cold green beans for breakfast and pack up.

Getting off the island is a reverse of what we did to get on it. Bag up our packs in garbage bags, blow up a couple of bags for flotation, and duct tape to each pack. Tie a rope between the two. I even stow my red Diamondback baseball cap in the pack, I don't want to lose that, even though I feel naked without it and my sandy brown hair is long enough to be falling into my eyes and quite annoying.

Down to skivvies again, we haul our stuff to the upstream end of the island and look. The guns are sealed in with the packs as well as my baseball bat, so we need to make sure there are no Zs here. This time, though, we both have knives belted to our waists.

It's light enough now that the sandstone along the river is like a grey moonscape and the layers of the canyon's cliffs are distant ghosts. We see no movement, we hear nothing beyond the roar of the river.

"It's gonna be cold," I say, already chilled from the air.

She smiles. "If it's the only indignity today, this'll be one for the record books."

"June, I..." I start, tugging on my beard nervously, needing to say things, but being too damn scared. Happy to take on a zombie, but scared to tell a woman how I feel.

"What? What is it?" She's looking around, her eyes wide, worried about danger again.

"No. There's nothing wrong." I touch her cool shoulder. "I... I just wanted to say, I'm really glad we met." And that's as close as I can get to saying what should be said.

"Me too," she says with a smile. "Ready?"

I nod and we walk into the freezing cold water. I curse. She laughs at me.

We're at the top of a big S in the river with a wide sandbar on the inside of that S-curve. We swim hard, dragging our gear, which floats nicely, and make it with ease. It's quiet on the other side, and we unwrap our packs, dress, and get going.

I get my hat back on and my jacket, checking the inside pocket, which I do a dozen times a day, and make sure my seed packets are still there. When every day is on the edge of survival, it seems like a silly dream—having a place to grow some food and maybe being a tiny bit normal. But since I escaped the mess in Phoenix and especially before I met June, this is the dream that kept me going.

We don't talk, we get our weapons out—June her gun, me my baseball bat, and set off. The Tonto Trail is up some rolling sandstone slick rock and soon we are heading northeast to Tanner Trail and our way out.

Not one Z sighting—this is looking like a good plan.

Not far down the trail, we're coming off the sandstone, down a steep section that is a bit of a scramble. We're getting close to the river again and that rapid that's just above the island.

"You'll be dropping your weapons now," a man says from behind a boulder, just off the trail. It's still not full light and I don't get a good look at him, but he has a bit of a southern twang to his voice.

We both freeze. June has her gun in her hand and I've got my bat. She's staring at him, doing the odds in her head, I am sure, and I think she would have tried, but—

"We gotcha covered," a woman says from the other side of the trail down a little, crouched behind another boulder. She's got a southern accent too.

June gives me a nod and drops her gun, slowly pulls her rifle from her shoulder and lowers it to the ground. I drop my bat and pull my pistol and put it on the ground.

"I guess we can't catch a break," I whisper.

"Now the knives," the man says, standing up and taking a step towards us, his pistol pointed at me.

"No," June says.

"I beg your pardon, young lady?" he says. He's shaggy and maybe forty with grey invading his brown beard and his long brown hair.

"No," she repeats. I'm freaking a bit, I don't know what she's up to. "There are Zs down here. We must be able to defend ourselves."

"You hear that, Mary," he says, glancing at the woman. "She thinks she gets ta keep her knife."

"Look," I say. "We are headed up the trail. We're leaving. We mean you no harm."

"Sorry there, boy," he says. "Orders are orders. All survivors come with us." He takes another step forward and levels his gun at me. He's five yards away and I am completely helpless. "Now, drop the knives."

We do as we're told. It's now clear that we are into psychotic, petty, wannabe warlord territory, and they are much more dangerous than zombies.

June changes her demeanor when she gives up the knife. Her shoulders are rounded and she steps close to me, her hand reaching for mine. Now, I've known her long enough to know this is an act.

The man talked to me first and is clearly underestimating June. She's playing in to that.

"Now cuff yourselves together," he says, tossing us a set of handcuffs. The woman, Mary, is close, her gun trained on us. She's tall and gangly and probably around forty like the man, with long black hair pulled back.

I try to catch June's eye, but she grabs the handcuffs and puts them on us, but loosely. She then holds my hand and squeezes it.

This is not good. Even if we could get away we would have no weapons and no supplies and would be handcuffed together.

They turn us around and we start heading downstream, away from Tanner Trail and our way out. They stay about ten feet behind us. They're not dumb. Most folks who have survived this long are not.

June doesn't speak, her jaw locked and her eyes taking in everything. I follow suit, looking for Zs, looking for opportunities, trying to figure out how to stay alive.

CHAPTER FOUR

"YOU KNOW," I say as we walk down the trail, our captors behind us, "we'll just slow you down if you're going back to Phantom Ranch. That is where you're from, isn't it? Just let us have our packs and you'll never see us again."

I can't see them, but I hear their boots scraping on the trail. The morning is warming, and I spot a few condors cruising in the updrafts high above.

"Watta y'all know about them zombies down here?" he asks.

"It's a zombie plague," I offer. "They are everywhere." There is no way I'm telling them that June and I did this.

He snorts. "We ain't seen but one or two until they started floating down the river a couple a days ago."

I shrug. "Forty miles is a long hike."

He chuckles. "Hear that, Mary? The boy thinks we're gonna hike all the way to The Ranch."

"Must be as dumb as he looks, Sal," she says.

We don't get anything else out of them except the confirmation that they are at Phantom Ranch.

They hike us about a mile and take us off the trail and down a drainage to the river. There's a grey river raft, about sixteen feet long, pulled up on the sand and tied off to a spindly tamarisk tree. There is an outboard motor on the back and the raft is just below a sizeable rapid, the air moist from the churning water.

I'm puzzled. Sure, we could float all the way down to Phantom Ranch from here—about ten miles on the river through some epic rapids—but we'd never get back up. How did they get that raft here?

Mary gives her gun to Sal and gets us into the raft and ties our handcuffs to the bowline. We could undo the knots, but it wouldn't be quick.

They push us off and down we go.

I can't say that I don't enjoy it some. In the old world, it was very difficult to get a private permit onto the Grand, and you had to know what you were doing. Or you could spend big bucks and buy your way down.

Yeah, we're handcuffed, and Mary has a gun on us while Sal rows us out into the current of the muddy river, but we're rafting down the Colorado.

We float for a while, the canyon walls becoming more sheer as the canyon deepens, cooler air floating off the cold water as the heat of the day starts to settle in.

Our captors don't talk much, and neither do June and I. What is there to say?

I hear the roar of a rapid coming, when Sal takes us into a sandy shore. They get us out, tie the boat off, and we're scrambling up a drainage back to the Tonto Trail.

And then I get it. They've got rafts staged along the river for the calm sections. They can float down and motor up. They hike around the rapids.

A half an hour later, my theory is confirmed when we come to a similar raft tied off below another rapid. After Mary ties us in, I whisper to June, "They're smart and well organized."

She nods. "That's what I'm worried about."

I settle in and do what I can to enjoy the journey, marveling at the deepening, dark grey inner gorge, the 1.5-billion-year-old Vishnu Schist. We've completed our journey down into the canyon and back through time—so to speak.

They hike us up and around the rapids, sometimes taking us far away from the river where we see the tan, brown, and salmon layers of rock all around us and the pointed temples of rock towering over us. Blue sky above, ravens cawing at us, signs of rabbit and coyote on the trail.

We spot Zs, mostly from the raft, but don't have any close encounters. Every time I see one, I feel a little pang of guilt. We did this. They kind of are *our* zombies.

June keeps her act up, holding my hand, leaning against me. I can't say I mind it at all, but it is definitely not June. I'm sure she can be affectionate, but I absolutely cannot see her as needy.

"Ain't these love birds cute," Sal says when we push off for the third time.

"Just like a couple o' precious doves," Mary says. "Ain't got a clue what Talia gonna do with these two. Probably a waste draggin' 'em all the way down."

June sucks in a breath, her brow furrowing in what looks like fear, and then shakes her head. A moment later, she squeezes my hand three times and I squeeze back. I get it. A strategy. If we appear to be useless maybe this Talia will let us go.

Soon it's early afternoon and we're back on our feet having spent several hours scrambling up one dry creek bed, walking on the relative flats above the inner gorge, and then scrambling down another.

I'm tired and my wrist is chafed from the hiking and the handcuffs. We've each only got one hand to climb with. We've taken to holding hands the whole time, despite them being sweaty, to reduce the chaffing, and keep the "love birds" thing going.

We aren't on the Toho Trail, but our way is marked by rock cairns. It's clear that they move up and down the river fairly freely. Hunting, maybe. Looking for the living in their territory, undoubtedly.

These scrambles are on both sides of the river, probably wherever they could find the drainages that got them around the rapids. They've gotten very difficult as the inner gorge has gotten deeper. At this point, they have a few crude ladders made out of logs and sun-bleached timber setup up and we are uncuffed just long enough to go up or down them.

Right after a ladder down a thirty-foot cliff, the creek bed starts to open and I hear the roar of a rapid. We saw it on the upstream end, and it was a doozy with huge standing waves and big holes ready to suck in your raft. It's taken us a couple of hours just to get around it.

At this point, I don't hate our captors yet. They act all superior, but they haven't been cruel. We've had plenty of water, but no food, but what's a little hunger these days?

As I get my first glimpse of the river, I hear the snarl of a zombie and then spot them. There's four of them. It's narrow here and they probably floated ashore and had no place to go.

They're a mess. Ripped clothes, dangling arms, one of them clearly has a broken leg and can't move very well. We stop and look back.

"No, no," Sal says from behind us. "Let's see what you two love birds are made of."

"Sal..." Mary says.

"Oh hush, woman, Talia ain't here and she's gonna want to know anyway. We need fighters not lovers."

Out of the corner of my eye, I catch an odd expression on June's face, but don't have time for it. "How about our knives?" I ask. The Zs have spotted us and are snarling and shambling toward us, all grey-eyed fungus-powered hunger, eager for a good meal and to spread their infection.

He chuckles, it's a cruel sound, and I officially hate him.

"Rocks," June says and we step forward, each of us finding one that fits well in our fists.

Two have good legs and move ahead, and we scramble over a

couple of rocks into a fairly narrow sandy section just wide enough for the two of us.

"There's something I should say," I begin as the Zs get closer. They look less like tourists now, having been torn up by the river and the rapids. Their clothing just dangles, as does some of their flesh where the river or the journey down here ripped it free. It's two men coming at us, one has an eye dangling out of the socket and the other's chest is caved in.

"I... You..." I can't get it out. I just can't.

"Later, we'll talk later," she hisses, her eyes focused on the Zs.

And then they're on us.

Rocks don't work as well as a knife to the eye, especially when you're attached to someone else. I used to play baseball, so my upper body strength is still good, but I'm working with my left hand. I get the eye dangler and hit him hard in the head with the rock and he falls back. June kicks chest-caved-in and he goes down. We jump forward and let our boots do the rest of the work.

The goo from the busted opened heads is gross, but it's the sound that's the worst. The snapping of bone, the squishing of their fungus heads. And the rotting-meat-decay smell assaults me and I wish I had the time to puke.

Then the next two are on us, a woman and a teenage boy. I miss the boy's head and land a blow on his shoulder and I hear a bone snap. He collapses against me and I go down to my knees. June crouches low and kicks, taking the woman's knee out with a sickening crunch, the woman falls forward and is on June. And then...

Hell, I'm not sure what happened, exactly. The adrenaline is flowing, the stench of the Zs making my eyes water, my nice day gone, the peaceful time on our sand island a distant memory. It's fight or flight and there is nowhere to run.

I hit, I knee, I shove, I grunt. I feel June pulling my hand and our sweaty grip slips and the handcuffs cut into our wrists.

The next thing I know, I'm standing and sweating and panting, my boot coming down over and over on the zombies who are a long ways past moving at this point.

"Enough," June says. She's doubled over and panting. "Enough." She grabs my hand and squeezes.

That jolts me out of it and I catch her blue eyes and give her a tired smile.

We check each other for bites and we don't, thankfully, find any. In a fight like that... well, you never know. I turn back and stare at our captors knowing that our "useless" act is shot. "Happy?"

"Well, you're a disgustin' mess," Sal says, referring to the stinking gore covering our arms, faces, and clothes, "but that'll do. You gotta rinse off before I let you in my boat."

The river is deep and swift here, but we kneel by the side and splash ourselves off. June catches my eye and nods downstream. She's asking if we should try to swim for it, but the sound of rapids echo through the canyon and I shake my head. The water is too cold, the rapids too fierce, and we are handcuffed together.

There's nothing we can do until we get to Phantom Ranch.

CHAPTER FIVE

IT'S one more short boat ride, a nasty scramble back up to Tonto Trail, and then four more hours of hiking to the South Kaibab Trail and then back down to the Colorado River. The inner gorge is just too deep here for the boat trick to work, even with the ladders.

There are two suspension bridges across the Colorado—one at the Kaibab Trail, which Tonto Trail eventually runs into, and one at the Bright Angel Trail. These are the only ways across the river by foot. As we come up to the Kaibab Suspension Bridge, the trail runs through a short tunnel and we all stop, taking a moment in the relative cool.

The bridge dangles above the river with metal railings and a wooden deck. It's just wide enough for the mules that used to come down here. And that's what I'm thinking when I step into a nice, fresh plop of mule crap.

Sal laughs and I just keep going. It's not much of an indignity as these things go. This is how they bring down supplies and gas for those rafts, they must have mules. I'm really not looking forward to this. They are way too well organized.

The north side of the bridge has a series of three chain-link gates that are as tall as the railings. The first two are easy to get through, just a simple latch, and are for the Zs. The last one is locked and manned, with razor wire on the top of it and two men guarding.

"Fresh meat," Sal says, and we're waved through.

The other side of the trail is cut into the cliff, but quickly flattens out and crosses the wide sandy delta of Bright Angel Creek.

On the west side of the delta are some buildings, they were set up for the mule teams, as I recall, and I can see the Bright Angel Suspension Bridge. We head up the trail, past the old campground which appears to be used for storage, towards Phantom Ranch which is up the creek a ways in an area of Bright Angel Canyon that flares out. It's early evening and there is already a lot of shade.

Phantom Ranch is nicely treed with a large dining hall, a few dormitories, and quaint cabins made out of sandstone rocks. I recall seeing deer wandering in at night when I was down here as a kid.

We both are exhausted and defeated. During our last encounter with a psychotic, petty, wannabe warlord, I had time to prepare a bluff that I used to get them to free June. This time? I got nothing.

They escort us into the dining hall. It's an open space with wood beams on the ceiling and lots of windows out the front. Most of the tables and chairs are stacked along the walls and two tables have been pushed together in the center. They're covered in papers and there are two men facing us and one woman facing away.

The hall is hot and smells of food, grilled onions and meat, reminding me just how hungry I am.

My eyes are drawn to the woman. She's tall, long sandy-blond hair contained in a ponytail with the sides of her head shaved. She's lean but muscular with a faded brown tank top on and lots of ink.

"Fresh meat, Boss," Sal says. The men only briefly looking at us and then back down at the papers.

June stiffens and sucks in a breath by my side and lets go of my hand. The woman, Talia it must be, straightens.

"Just a couple o' love birds," he continues. "But I must say they are scrappy. Found 'em up towards Tanner Trail hidin' from them zombies in that sandbar in the middle of the river. Say they don't know about 'em, but you wouldn't swim the river if you weren't being chased by a bunch."

Talia turns and her brown eyes go right to June and her jaw falls open. I glance at June and she is blinking and biting her lip.

"Oh, my dear, sweet Jesus..." Talia says as she steps forward. "June Medina. I... I thought you died. I thought you..." Talia blinks, her hand coming to her slack face and her eyes water up. She looks at the handcuffs and our badly scraped wrists. "Sal, you get her out of those cuffs this second, or I swear..."

Sal moves quickly and uncuffs June, but leaves my cuff untouched. "Sorry, ma'am. Protocol, you know," he says, the gruff man suddenly cowering.

At this point, it was like I wasn't there. June and Talia are staring at each other and you could just about power a blender with the electricity passing between them.

"If I found you've treated them badly..." Talia says, not even looking at Sal. Her voice is fairly deep and she speaks loudly.

"It's been a fine day," I say, eyeing Sal. "Just a nice float down the river and an easy hike." But I don't think they even hear me.

Talia takes another step forward and her hands are shaking. June's face is hard, but she's blinking rapidly. I'm desperately trying to figure this out. They know each other. They were together after the Zs. And—

Talia shouts, "Jesus be praised and Gaia too!" and rushes up and grabs June, picks her up, and kisses her hard.

Ah... they were "together" after the Zs, as in a couple, as in... OK. Well, there's one mystery solved. I now know that June likes girls and I'm not even in the running.

CHAPTER SIX

AT FIRST, it's a relief. I can give up my romantic fantasies and get back to focusing on survival. While I don't know if Talia is a psychotic, petty, wannabe warlord or not, I'm reasonably confident that because of their connection, we're safe.

But then I notice that it's mostly Talia doing the kissing and June is stiff, her eyes wide.

Talia puts her down. And June wipes her mouth and then smiles awkwardly.

"Jesus! I mean, I swear. Jesus!" Talia says. "How'd you get from Albuquerque over here? What the hell happened at that market? How'd you escape?"

Everyone is staring now. The two men at the table, and Sal and Mary, but Talia seems oblivious.

June swallows. "Tal, this is my good friend Woody." She steps over, giving me a shy smile but briefly widens her eyes. She takes my hand, squeezes it, and adds, "We're... well, we're together now."

And yeah, my heart jumps into my throat, and I suck in some spit and start coughing hard. "Water..." I gasp.

"Jesus, Sal," Talia says. "I swear I'm gonna have to kick your ass again. Get the man some water and get them some food. Go!"

My eyes are watering and I look up to see Talia giving me an appraising look like she's sizing up a side of beef. "Sorry about that kiss..." Talia says, sounding shy but looking defiant. "It's just... well... Our June here is special."

I nodded, my voice a croak. "I couldn't agree more. I'd be lost without her."

Sal brings us water and some stew and takes the handcuff off my wrist. I gulp the water, which helps the coughing, and then we sit down and eat, while Talia goes on about Jesus and Gaia, pacing about the dining hall like it's the oval office, going on and on about the "miracle" of having June back.

We both eat, although I see June keeping a wary eye on Talia. She doesn't say much and I don't say anything. I don't ask about the chewy meat in the stew, I'm so happy to eat.

After our meal, we get the tour and it's impressive. With us, they've got fifty-five people here and it's well protected. On the south is the Colorado River. To the north where the canyon narrows in an area called "The Box" they've put up a barbed wire fence and have guards posted 24/7. They have another fence just north of Phantom Ranch which is much wider and harder to protect. Down by the river, near the mule stables and the Bright Angel Bridge, they're gardening and even have two mules.

I learn a bit of pre-apocalypse history during the tour. June and Talia met while serving in Afghanistan. Not Army Rangers, but Army, so I was close on that. They were visiting Talia's parents in Albuquerque when the Zs happened.

"The Ranch," as they call it, is ideal. Protected. Isolated. All the water you need. A bit hot, but that just helps keep people away.

It's nearly dark once the tour is over and Talia escorts us to a cabin. "There's water inside and a little food. Some first aid stuff for your wrists. Make yourselves at home." She pauses then and stares at

June. "Jesus Christ, June-bug. I'm just so glad to have you back." She gives June a fierce hug. "May Gaia be praised!"

When we get inside, June's eyes are wide and she grabs me and hisses in my ear, her breath warm. "She's crazy. We have to get out of here."

CHAPTER SEVEN

THE CABIN HAS food and water, both for drinking and for cleaning up, and our jackets. There's even some Neosporin and bandages. It doesn't, though, have our packs or any weapons.

"God, I'm wiped out, honey," June says after she lets me go, her eyes wide again. "I could sleep for a year."

I open my fat mouth to ask her what she's talking about and she puts her hand on my lips and shakes her head and then points to her ear and then outside. They might be listening?

I think about it, and yeah, they might. Small battery-powered electronics, why not? We used that kind of thing all the time in the Phoenix group I was with.

"Me too," I say. "My blisters are back, my wrist is killing me, and I'm exhausted, but this place is amazing." I rattle on for a while about how amazing things are at "The Ranch."

June takes her boots off and tiptoes around the place looking at everything. It's just one room with a bed, a small desk, a chair, and a bathroom with a groover in it. A groover is a toilet seat on top of a big ammo can lined with a bag, the kind of toilet setup used by river runners.

I pull my boots off and lie back on the bed with a groan. A real bed. I don't even know how long it's been since I've slept in a real bed. It's soft, but that softness just feels foreign.

June bounces down next to me and is whispering in my ear again, her warm breath and her familiar scent waking me up. "She was always high strung, but a good soldier. We were on leave from active duty when it came down... she... she. She lost it. She'll never let me go. I faked my death back in Albuquerque to get away." June ends in a shrug. "Oh, sweetie," she says looking at my wrist and feet. "Let me clean those up for you."

We spend the next hour switching between banal conversation, tending to our wounds, and whispering in each other's ears. We have no supplies. We're in a well-guarded compound with only two ways out.

We'll never get across the bridge with its gates and guards, so that leaves a thirteen-mile hike north up the Kaibab Trail to the North Rim or stealing a raft and heading down the Colorado towards Lake Mead with absolutely no river running experience.

Yup. This is an ideal location... to get trapped.

CHAPTER EIGHT

THEY CALL THIS PLACE "THE RANCH." The organization is militaristic. Talia is in charge, although she has no rank. Her middle managers are called lieutenants. The whole group is referred to as "Phantom Company."

As it turns out, I can't sleep in a bed anymore and neither can June. It's just too soft. We ended up dragging the bedding down onto the floor around midnight and I am sleeping like the dead... no, that's not right, the dead roam the planet looking to consume the living now. Okay, I'm sleeping like a baby, when I am woken up by a trumpet playing reveille at 5:00 a.m.

"What the..." I mumble, rubbing at my eyes. My wrist is a scabby mess and my feet are killing me.

"Come on, sweetie," June says, sitting next to me, she's already dressed. "We need to get out there."

I blink and look at her and she has a sweet smile on her face, her short black hair is damp, so she just must have washed up. Her blue eyes... God, I'm getting used to them. And for a moment, just a moment, I forget that she's pretending that we're together just in case someone is listening. I forget that we're trapped under the leadership of an unstable personality that is obsessed with June and would probably be happy to see me out of the picture by any means.

"Good morning, beautiful," I say, my smile going from wide to nervous as all this tumbles down on me. Her eyebrows dance briefly, her forehead crinkles, and I swear I see her blush before she turns away.

"Hurry up," she says, turning her back to me. "Get dressed. We've got to get out there."

Phantom Company has a boot-camp style gathering at 5:15 a.m. Including some calisthenics, duty assignments, and a few words from Talia.

Yeah, besides being trapped, this makes this place seem a whole lot less ideal. The exercise is fine, I'm in decent shape from running away from Zs, but I don't like the assignments.

A guy that goes by Harris, a buzzed cut, middle-aged, muscly, military sort, rattles off changes in duty assignments. He was one of the men we first saw with Talia. I'm to report to Meryl, a fifty-year-old man with a greying ponytail who runs the kitchen and farm, and June is to report to... wait for it... Talia. Her assignment is not clear. June's standing at attention and looking straight ahead, so I can't get a read on her.

I count forty-nine of us in front of the dining hall lined up in four straight lines. That leaves six people out on sentry duty. Ages vary from around fifteen to seventy. Most people have a knife on their belt, but the only guns visible are Talia and her lieutenants, and presumably the guards.

After Harris is done, Talia struts in front of "the company," her hands clasped behind her back, still dressed in that tank top despite the cool morning. The tattoo on her left arm is of a skull with a snake running through the eye.

"We've got two new members to our company," she says, stopping in front of us and smiling. "June Medina and Woody..." she gives me a questioning look.

"Beckman," I say, doing my best to smile.

"...and Woody Beckman. June served with me and we are lucky to have them. I want you all to help them acclimate to things down here on The Ranch."

She begins pacing again and takes a deep breath, her voice strengthening. "Every day down here, every task we do, we do for the survival of the human race. Each job is important. Each member of our team invaluable. Each day a victory. With the help of Jesus above and Gaia below, we will not only survive, we will thrive!"

She ends square in front of the group and raises her arms into the air and shouts, "Phantom Company!"

The call is echoed by the people around me. I'm standing there with my jaw hanging loose like some fool. She mentioned Gaia. When I offered my time travel theory about the origins of the zombie infections, June countered with a Gaia theory—that the planet had created the fungal parasite to keep us from destroying it. A shiver runs through me.

Talia pumps her arms again and everyone yells "Phantom Company." I notice June is enthusiastically yelling, and I just want to freak. The third time I join in, just so I don't stand out.

After mess, which consisted of oatmeal and dried fruit, June kisses me on the check and says, "See you later, honey," before following Talia, Harris, Sal, and another woman outside.

I sit staring at the door. Maybe this weird Jesus, Gaia thing is the way June is. She used to be with Talia. Maybe she'll want to go back to her, maybe she'll...

I shake it off. She's terrified of Talia—June being terrified of someone is a terrible thought—and that's why she just called me honey and kissed me on the cheek.

My mind is running rampant on the June and Talia thing when a thirtyish woman walks into the building, a tired look on her round face. She's tall and pretty with shoulder-length brown hair and has a gun on her hip. She must be one of the sentries, probably coming off shift.

Her eyes meet mine as she strides through the room. She tucks her hair behind her ear and smiles as she looks me over.

It's *that* kind of smile. I smile back, unsure what to think, most of the looks I've gotten have been guarded or curious stares that last a rudely long time.

I watch her walk back into the kitchen where she's handed a tray with some food. She sits down a few tables away and smiles at me again. Is she flirting?

"Come on, Beckman. Time to get to work."

I look up, it's Meryl waving me back towards the kitchen. I shake off the thoughts of June and her ex and this new woman. Time for my first day as part of Phantom Company.

CHAPTER NINE

THE DAY SPINS by with half in the hot kitchen working on tonight's dinner stew, made from some old potatoes with a lot of eyes, canned vegetables, and some dried mystery meat—I'd rather not know what. The other half of the day is out in the sun weeding and hauling water by hand from the Colorado to water the plants.

Meryl moves slow and talks slow and speaks in a monotone and doesn't get any of my jokes. I don't know how long I can do this. To be clear, the work is fine, it's the lack of laughter that will do me in. I've got my two goals for the day, survival and laughter, and need them both.

The day ends in the dining hall, cleaning up after mess, and I still haven't seen June, or Talia for that matter. This is only day ten for us, but I feel incomplete without her. I don't like it at all. I spent the whole day thinking I was forgetting to do something.

When I stumble back to our cabin, exhausted, I am delighted to see her there.

"God, you are a sight for sore eyes," I say.

She's sitting on the edge of the bed, her eyes downcast, chewing on her lip. She nods and says, "You are too, babe." Her voice is light, but her face is not. Something is wrong.

She pats on the bed next to her and I flop down with a sigh and take a deep breath. "Tough work, but they've got a great setup here," I say, just in case they are listening.

"Yeah," she says. "Talia has done well. Amazing, really."

She then grabs me, her lips brushing my ear and a chill runs down my spine and I'm suddenly awake. "You're not safe."

"Meryl is a good guy," I say, my eyes wide. "I can see why they are glad to have us. They definitely need more hands."

We go on like this, talking about how wonderful The Ranch is and whispering in each other's ears.

Talia got June alone today and made her case as to why June needs to leave me and come back to her. How together they will be the ones to "save the human race." Asked her how well she knew me, asked her if she could even trust me. Told her that I didn't seem like her type. Told her she has seen guys like me before and I couldn't be trusted.

At this point, I'm not at all sure what June's type is. All I know is that Talia was once her type and that I don't like Talia one bit.

And true believers, don't get me started on them and people with missions to save this world. I barely escaped from one in Phoenix. I understand how in these desperate times it's easy to fall prey to someone who is so confident in themselves. But it's not real. They're either full of it, or nuts, or both.

June told Talia that we are in love, that I am "the one," that she is sure about me. Talia tried to kiss her again, got aggressive, it might have gone bad if Harris hadn't walked in.

I'm up and pacing, my fatigue forgotten. I'm angry. I want my baseball bat and a good-sized group of Zs to take on. I'm having trouble keeping up the charade. I want to go out into the night right now and march down to Talia's cabin, it's one of the big ones that families stayed in. I want to...

June gets up, grabs me, and holds me tight. She's afraid and that is... I don't even know how to describe it. On one hand, this beautiful, tough-ass woman is afraid and seems to want me to comfort her. On the other hand, one of the most competent people I've met in the post-apocalyptic world is afraid and... well, that's not good.

"There was a girl in Albuquerque," she whispers in my ear, "that liked me. Not even a real flirtation, and..." She ends shaking her head and won't say more.

"We need to leave," I whisper back. "Even if it doesn't work, we have to try."

She nods.

"Still got your lighter?" While they took our packs and our weapons, they didn't search our pockets. She always has a lighter with her.

"Yes," she whispers.

"Then I have an idea."

We spend the next hour working it out.

THERE'S a lot I hate about this plan of ours. It puts some good people at risk, but there doesn't seem to be another way. It is, though, the first plan that we've made together, so it's bound to go great, right?

Here's the problem. We're in a well-protected, isolated area at the bottom of the Grand Canyon in an armed compound run by a woman obsessed with June. All we have is what is in our pockets and what is in the room. June has a lighter and a small pocketknife. I've got a compass, a beat-up map of the Grand Canyon trails, and a small Leatherman multi-tool.

I have a brief moment when I realize I forgot about the Leatherman when we battled the Zs, but only briefly. It's too small to be effective.

If we do escape, we could encounter zombies, we could be chased, and we will most certainly be challenged by the elements.

In the room, we have some first aid supplies: hydrogen peroxide,

Neosporin, and some bandages. Plus, there's three power bars, soap, toothpaste, and toothbrushes, a small LED lantern, and two bottles of water.

That's it.

We use the scissors on the Leatherman and cut two long, wide strips from the sheet. With this we can roll things up in them, tie them at the ends and sling it all over our shoulders so we can carry a few things. The rest of the sheets we cut into smaller strips, knot them together, and fashion a bit of rope.

Using a bunch of the cotton bandaging, toilet paper, and wood shavings, we set up a fire.

It's a bit of a Rube Goldberg machine with a small fire in a trash can that will jump to the bandaging and climb up onto the chair and ignite a larger fire, which will then connect with the drapes and involve the entire cabin.

We need a delay before the whole cabin is in flames.

See why I hate the plan? I don't really want to burn down Phantom Ranch, but we need a distraction and we need everyone to be busy.

June is the firebug and is sure that the chained fires will work.

After prep, we turn off the lights and lie down, waiting for everyone else to fall asleep. She takes my hand and squeezes it. I squeeze back. My stomach is roiling and my brain won't stop freaking out and is going over and over our plan endlessly.

At 2:00 a.m. she lights the fire, we tie our makeshift sacks on, grab the rope we made out of sheets, and sneak out.

CHAPTER TEN

THERE ARE high clouds and the night is dark. It's quiet except for the babbling of Bright Angel Creek. We go low and head east to the steep slopes of this side canyon and then head north.

I follow June's lead. We go in short spurts, hiding behind trees, watching. My eyes adjust quickly and it gets easier.

We make our way a few hundred feet north until we're in sight of the first, wider fence. Our cover is good and we spot the single sentry. It's a man, not the woman I saw after breakfast.

The fence runs from the edge of the creek to the canyon wall. This fence can't really protect the entire area like the one up at The Box can.

We wait. Five minutes and I'm thinking the fire didn't take. The guard is bored, walking on the trail, kicking at the dirt. Yawning.

Ten minutes and I'm about to lose it. I look at June, but she's focused on the guard. We have a plan B, but I don't like it.

Fifteen minutes, and it's time for plan B. June gets up to go pretend she couldn't sleep and then take the guard out, but I catch a whiff of smoke and grab her.

Soon we hear the crackling, but the camp is still quiet. The guard is whistling now, looking to the north and not seeing the flicker of flames behind us.

June grabs a rock and tosses it, making enough noise to catch his attention. He sees the fire, curses, and runs down the trail. There are shouts from behind us. Once the guard is out of sight, we run, get through the gate, and keep running.

ⵉ 𐤉 ⵉ

WE ARE NORTH of the first fence, and its distractible guard and distracted camp, but south of the better fence with guards we can't distract. They have guns, we don't. There is only one other trail here, Clear Creek Trail, that starts just north of Phantom Ranch and heads to the east nine miles, ending at Clear Creek in the depths of the Grand Canyon.

Right before the trail, we drink our water bottles dry, refill them from the creek, and head up. We have no choice.

We climb up the switchbacks as quickly as we can, up and out of the river gorge. The trail then goes east and parallels the river for a while and we go down that way a few hundred yards, dropping some threads from our sheets for pursuers to find. We then backtrack, going most of the way back down and head cross-country to the north.

The backtracking is risky. We need them to waste time on Clear Creek Trail and we're betting that the fire will keep them busy long enough for us to do this.

Clear Creek is no good. We would get trapped there.

Bushwhacking across the Grand Canyon is not what we want, but we have to get out. The North Rim is the only way. It's slow going in the dark, but we scramble slowly and carefully. We're just on top of the first steep climb up out of Bright Angel Canyon, a few hundred feet above the creek.

Not the type of hike anyone takes on willingly, much less in the dark. The flickering light from the south and the whiff of smoke makes me feel guilty until I think of Talia. She forced us into this situation. She brought this on.

It's slow, dangerous going, but we scramble along, just above the steepest part of the cliff. Around The Box, it's nearly impassable and we slow way down using our sheet-rope. One of us sits anchored and the other one carefully crawls forward. We eventually get past The Box and the north-most fence.

We make some noise—even going slow and trying not to, we make noise. Each bump, each slip, each rock skittering down is like a blow. We're just hoping that they are busy and distracted by the fire.

We find a reasonable slope, which means only scrapes and bruises, and make it down to Bright Angel Trail.

Once down, we just squat there, catching our breath and listening. We're both sweaty and exhausted and very thirsty, but we don't move. Not for ten minutes.

It's silent, so we drink a little water, exchange a quick smile in the gloomy dark, and head to the north.

We don't have much food, but the trail parallels Bright Angel Creek much of the way so we'll have water. I feel a lightness about me and am about to open my mouth to say something when I hear the unmistakable snick-click of a pistol being cocked.

CHAPTER ELEVEN

"HERE'S THE THING, JUNE-BUG," Talia says as she paces in front of us. "Did you not think about walkie talkies, or did you just assume the fire would consume all of our attention?"

I hate that nickname. It implies that June is small, and she might be in stature, but not in spirit. I can't imagine what June thinks of it. And Talia left out the third option, "you're so damned desperate to get away from me that you'd try anything."

Sal and Harris have their guns pointed at us and there are a few flashlights providing some illumination. June's got my hand and is squeezing it hard.

"A daring escape, I'll give you that," Talia continues. "But the guards heard you up above and we had plenty of time to deal with the fire and get up here before you." She shakes her head, her ponytail wagging behind her. "Not good enough. I expect better from you."

She sighs in an annoyingly psychotic, petty, wannabe warlord way. "In any case, you'll be coming back with us now. You'll be made a nice example of. Both of you. Let's move."

Neither of us have spoken a word. Talia had to give her tiresome, warlord speech before anything else could happen. June is terrified and not herself. I've had zero time to prep, but there is one card I can play. A big fat bluff, but maybe it will wake June up.

"Hold on," I say, holding up my hand. "I think you can spare me a moment and let me explain why you're going to let us go." Sure, I sound like I know what I'm talking about, but my heart is pounding out an insanely fast rhythm in my head and I'm making this up as I go.

June gives my hand a desperate squeeze, as if to ask me what the hell I'm doing, or maybe to beg me to shut up. I have no idea. And sure, I could get us killed now, but, hey, that might be better than being "made a nice example of."

"Very well," she says. "Dazzle me." She injects enough sarcasm that I want to punch her.

"You've got a good thing going here," I nod back to Phantom Ranch. "If you had given us a choice, we would have happily taken our packs and been on our way, but you didn't do that."

She waves her hand at me impatiently. I'm stalling and she knows it.

"June and I are in love," I tell her and turn to June and meet her eyes. "I've been a goner since the first day we met. There is no life for me now without her."

It's fairly dark, but I can see how wide June's eyes are.

And then it clicks. I know what might work.

I turn back to the impatient Talia. "And she's told me everything. What happened in Afghanistan. How things went to shit in Albuquerque." And now I'm in complete bullshit land. I mean, I know things went down, something happened to the girl that had a crush on June. I know there are things Talia's done that she's not proud of, provided she's not a complete psychopath.

"You've got a whole new crew that respects you," I say. "It's going great. So, you can let us go now," I say with a smile. "Or we can start talking."

She's breathing heavy and steps forward and presses her pistol to my forehead. "Or, I can just kill you both now," she says.

June is squeezing my hand so hard it hurts. I slowly shake my head, careful not to dislodge or jostle the gun. "No. You can't." And yes, I'm still bullshitting my ass off and would have pissed my pants if I hadn't been fairly dehydrated. "You can kill me, sure, but I know you can't kill June. Not our special June. And she'll spill the whole way back, tell everyone there exactly what your past looks like, even before the Zs."

I can see her eyes and she is furious, her nostrils flaring, her jaw locked. And I wasn't lying when I said she had a good thing back there. The gamble I'm taking is that it's more important to her than proving something here.

The seconds tick past and I just know it's not enough. She's going to pull the trigger.

"Please," June whispers. "Tal. Please. For the good times we had. For the love we shared. Please let us go."

She cocks the gun and I swear to God I can hear her teeth grinding. I squeeze June's hand and I'm sweating like it's midday and I just ran a 10k. She's going to do it.

And then... Talia blinks and slowly nods her head, the gun falling to her side, her shoulders slumping.

I think we can drop the petty from my description of Talia, so now she's only a "psychotic, wannabe warlord."

She stumbles down the trail and doesn't look back. "Give them your guns and knives," she calls back to the two men. "And anything you have to eat. Let them go. Now."

"But... Talia," Sal says.

Talia stops and even in the gloom I can see how high her shoulders are. "I swear to God, Sal, those two gave me a good reason not to kill them. Have you?"

CHAPTER TWELVE

AFTER THEY'RE GONE we don't move. We're just standing there holding hands, my whole body is shaking, sweat dripping down my back. I hear the water rushing down the creek and cicadas buzzing in the night. I can't believe it worked. I feel... so tired, so weak, and yet I feel invincible. We just talked Talia down. We've got weapons now. They're not going to chase us. I feel this strange high.

"I meant what I said," I whisper, that manic energy finally getting me to open my mouth.

"What?" June asks.

"I have been a goner since the first day we met. There is no life for me now without you."

I don't turn. I can't. I feel her looking at me, but I'm terrified to look at her. Bullshit an armed psychotic, wannabe warlord? Sure. Face rejection from June head-on? Nope.

She doesn't speak for the longest time and I'm half-convinced that she's going to go running back to Talia.

"It's..." she begins, swallowing hard. "You know, it's..."

I turn to her. "I know it's complicated, June. We are barely surviving, how safe is it to feel like this about someone when we have no idea what tomorrow will bring?"

She nods.

"And if being your friend and your partner out here is all I get... I'm... I'm good with that."

"Okay..." she says, biting her lip. She takes a deep breath, nods her head, and says "Okay" again, but resolutely this time. She lets go of my hand and gathers up the gear the men left us just like it's business as usual. She divvies it up and gets on the trail.

When we've been on the trail for a while and it's starting to get light, I just can't stand it anymore. "So... just to be clear, you like girls *and* guys. Right?" She must. She was with Talia, but Talia bought her being with me.

She stops and stares at me.

"I just need to know if there's a chance. Is there?"

Her blue eyes bore into me, a smile playing on her lips.

"Tell you what," she says. "I'll let you know when we reach the top and have a safe place to rest." She turns and trots up the trail.

"Seriously?" I yell after her. "I mean, seriously!?"

Her laughter bounces off the canyon walls and I happily chase her up the trail.

EPISODE 5

WOODY AND JUNE VERSUS THE THIRD WHEEL

More adventure, a poorly timed third wheel, and a lot more Woody and June awaits you in.... *Woody and June versus the June versus the Third Wheel.*

Coming soon on July 10, 2019

Join the Woody and June Fan Club at WoodyAndJune.com so you don't miss a thing (plus fun behind-the-scenes features and free stuff!).

ᛚᛐᚾ ᛐᚾ ᛐᛐᛐ

WOODY AND JUNE VERSUS THE THIRD WHEEL

Him and Her and... Her?

When Woody Beckman meets June Medina, neither expects the adventures that will follow. Dedicated go-it-alone survivors, they've learned not to trust anyone in post-zombie-apocalypse Arizona, except each other.

There's nothing harder on a new romance than a third wheel.

Finally free of immediate danger, Woody and June must contend with a mysterious stranger whose intentions are not at all clear.

Can Woody and June's growing relationship survive the devious third wheel?

A story of adventure and love and taking things (even the apocalypse) in stride.

ABOUT THE AUTHOR

Robert J. McCarter is the author of six novels, three novellas, and dozens of short stories. He is a finalist for the *Writers of the Future* contest and his stories have appeared in *The Saturday Evening Post, Adomeda Spaceways Inflight Magazine, Everyday Fiction,* and numerous anthologies.

He has written a series of first person ghost novels (starting with Shuffled Off: A Ghost's Memoir) and a superhero / love story series (Neutrinoman and Lightningirl, A Love Story), as well as two short story collections.

Of his latest novel, *Seeing Forever,* Kirkus Reviews says, "Sci-fi as it should be: engaging, moving, and grand in scope."

Find out more at:
robertjmccarter.com

BOOKS BY ROBERT J. MCCARTER

WOODY AND JUNE VERSUS THE APOCALYPSE

1. Woody and June versus the Wannabe Warlord
2. Woody and June versus the Fungus-Head Zombies
3. Woody and June versus the Grand Canyon
4. Woody and June versus the Ex
5. Woody and June versus the Third Wheel (*coming July, 2019*)
6. Woody and June versus Phantom Company (*coming August, 2019*)
7. Woody and June versus the Daring Rescue (*coming September, 2019*)

Join the Woody and June Fan Club at WoodyAndJune.com

NOVELS IN THE "GHOST'S MEMOIR" WORLD:

- Shuffled Off: A Ghost's Memoir, Book 1
- Drawing the Dead
- To Be a Fool: A Ghost's Memoir, Book 2
- Of Things Not Seen: A Ghost's Memoir, Book 3

OTHER NOVELS:

- Seeing Forever

BOOKS IN THE NEUTRINOMAN AND LIGHTNINGIRL SERIES:

- Meteor Attack! Neutrinoman and Lightningirl, A Love Story. Episode 1
- Toxic Asset: Neutrinoman and Lightningirl, A Love Story. Episode 2
- Protocol X: Neutrinoman and Lightningirl, A Love Story. Episode 3
- Season 1 (Omnibus edition of Episodes 1 - 3)
- Off Book: Neutrinoman and Lightningirl, A Love Story. Episode 4 (*Coming soon*)

WALTER ANCHOR, GHOST DETECTIVE STORIES

- **Case 1: "Detecting Haley"** (part of *Life After: Stories of Life, Death, and the Places in Between*)
- **Case 2: "The Ghost Brides Gift"** (exclusive to newsletter subscribers)
- **Case 3: "A Long Hard Fall"** (coming in 2019)

For a complete list of Walter Anchor stories, go to RobertJMcCarter.com/WalterAnchor

SHORT STORES AND COLLECTIONS

- Life After: Stories of Life, Death, and the Places in Between
- Anomalous Readings: Thirteen Curious and Confounding Tales
- Probability: Resolve
- The Turing Test Will Be Televised

- Ghost Hacker, Zombie Maker

For a complete list, go to RobertJMcCarter.com